Times-Tables

This book belongs to

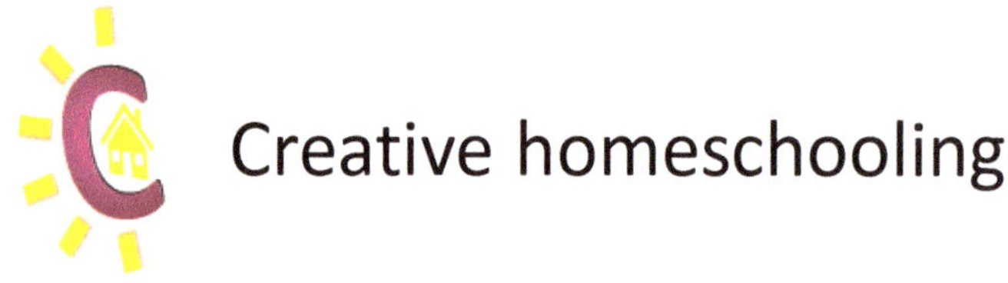

www.gajabooks.com

$$1 \times 1 = 1$$
$$1 \times 2 = 2$$
$$1 \times 3 = 3$$
$$1 \times 4 = 4$$
$$1 \times 5 = 5$$
$$1 \times 6 = 6$$
$$1 \times 7 = 7$$
$$1 \times 8 = 8$$
$$1 \times 9 = 9$$
$$1 \times 10 = 10$$

$$2 \times 1 = 2$$
$$2 \times 2 = 4$$
$$2 \times 3 = 6$$
$$2 \times 4 = 8$$
$$2 \times 5 = 10$$
$$2 \times 6 = 12$$
$$2 \times 7 = 14$$
$$2 \times 8 = 16$$
$$2 \times 9 = 18$$
$$2 \times 10 = 20$$

3 x 1 = 3

3 x 2 = 6

3 x 3 = 9

3 x 4 = 12

3 x 5 = 15

3 x 6 = 18

3 x 7 = 21

3 x 8 = 24

3 x 9 = 27

3 x 10 = 30

4

$$4 \times 1 = 4$$
$$4 \times 2 = 8$$
$$4 \times 3 = 12$$
$$4 \times 4 = 16$$
$$4 \times 5 = 20$$
$$4 \times 6 = 24$$
$$4 \times 7 = 28$$
$$4 \times 8 = 32$$
$$4 \times 9 = 36$$
$$4 \times 10 = 40$$

$$5 \times 1 = 5$$
$$5 \times 2 = 10$$
$$5 \times 3 = 15$$
$$5 \times 4 = 20$$
$$5 \times 5 = 25$$
$$5 \times 6 = 30$$
$$5 \times 7 = 35$$
$$5 \times 8 = 40$$
$$5 \times 9 = 45$$
$$5 \times 10 = 50$$

6

6 x 1 = 6
6 x 2 = 12
6 x 3 = 18
6 x 4 = 24
6 x 5 = 30
6 x 6 = 36
6 x 7 = 42
6 x 8 = 48
6 x 9 = 54
6 x 10 = 60

$$7 \times 1 = 7$$
$$7 \times 2 = 14$$
$$7 \times 3 = 21$$
$$7 \times 4 = 28$$
$$7 \times 5 = 35$$
$$7 \times 6 = 42$$
$$7 \times 7 = 49$$
$$7 \times 8 = 56$$
$$7 \times 9 = 63$$
$$7 \times 10 = 70$$

$$8 \times 1 = 8$$
$$8 \times 2 = 16$$
$$8 \times 3 = 24$$
$$8 \times 4 = 32$$
$$8 \times 5 = 40$$
$$8 \times 6 = 48$$
$$8 \times 7 = 56$$
$$8 \times 8 = 64$$
$$8 \times 9 = 72$$
$$8 \times 10 = 80$$

9

$$9 \times 1 = 9$$
$$9 \times 2 = 18$$
$$9 \times 3 = 27$$
$$9 \times 4 = 36$$
$$9 \times 5 = 45$$
$$9 \times 6 = 54$$
$$9 \times 7 = 63$$
$$9 \times 8 = 72$$
$$9 \times 9 = 81$$
$$9 \times 10 = 90$$

10 x 1 = 10
10 x 2 = 20
10 x 3 = 30
10 x 4 = 40
10 x 5 = 50
10 x 6 = 60
10 x 7 = 70
10 x 8 = 80
10 x 9 = 90
10 x 10 = 100

11 x 1 = 11
11 x 2 = 22
11 x 3 = 33
11 x 4 = 44
11 x 5 = 55
11 x 6 = 66
11 x 7 = 77
11 x 8 = 88
11 x 9 = 99
11 x 10 = 110

12 x 1 = 12
12 x 2 = 24
12 x 3 = 36
12 x 4 = 48
12 x 5 = 60
12 x 6 = 72
12 x 7 = 84
12 x 8 = 96
12 x 9 = 108
12 x 10 = 120

13 x 1 = 13

13 x 2 = 26

13 x 3 = 39

13 x 4 = 52

13 x 5 = 65

13 x 6 = 78

13 x 7 = 91

13 x 8 = 104

13 x 9 = 117

13 x 10 = 130

14	x 1	=	14
14	x 2	=	28
14	x 3	=	42
14	x 4	=	56
14	x 5	=	70
14	x 6	=	84
14	x 7	=	98
14	x 8	=	112
14	x 9	=	126
14	x 10	=	140

15

15 x 1 = 15
15 x 2 = 30
15 x 3 = 45
15 x 4 = 60
15 x 5 = 75
15 x 6 = 90
15 x 7 = 105
15 x 8 = 120
15 x 9 = 135
15 x 10 = 150

16 x 1 = 16

16 x 2 = 32

16 x 3 = 48

16 x 4 = 64

16 x 5 = 80

16 x 6 = 96

16 x 7 = 112

16 x 8 = 128

16 x 9 = 144

16 x 10= 160

17

17 x 1 = 17
17 x 2 = 34
17 x 3 = 51
17 x 4 = 68
17 x 5 = 85
17 x 6 = 102
17 x 7 = 119
17 x 8 = 136
17 x 9 = 153
17 x 10 = 170

18

18	x	1	=	18
18	x	2	=	36
18	x	3	=	54
18	x	4	=	72
18	x	5	=	90
18	x	6	=	108
18	x	7	=	126
18	x	8	=	144
18	x	9	=	162
18	x	10	=	180

19	x	1	=	19
19	x	2	=	38
19	x	3	=	57
19	x	4	=	76
19	x	5	=	95
19	x	6	=	114
19	x	7	=	133
19	x	8	=	152
19	x	9	=	171
19	x	10	=	190

20 x 1 = 20
20 x 2 = 40
20 x 3 = 60
20 x 4 = 80
20 x 5 = 100
20 x 6 = 120
20 x 7 = 140
20 x 8 = 160
20 x 9 = 180
20 x 10 = 200

YouTube

Creative homeschooling

practice
practice
practice
practice

www.gajabooks.com

Match the right answer to each calculation

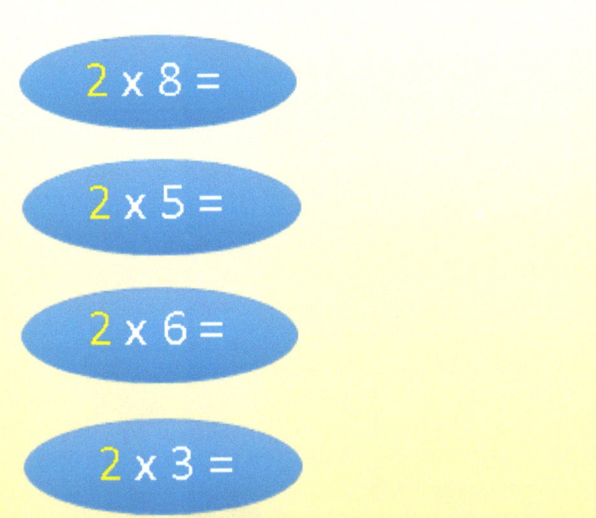

Multiple the number in the middle of each target by the numbers in the middle blue ring. Write your answers in the outside yellow ring.

Match the right answer to each calculation

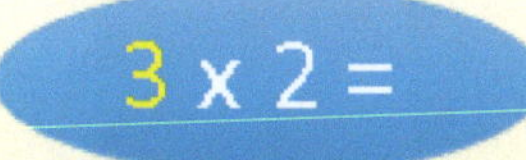

3 x 2 =	21
3 x 7 =	15
3 x 4 =	18
3 x 9 =	12
3 x 5 =	6

Multiple the number in the middle of each target by the numbers in the middle blue ring. Write your answers in the outside yellow ring.

Match the right answer to each calculation

Multiple the number in the middle of each target by the numbers in the middle blue ring. Write your answers in the outside yellow ring.

Match the right answer to each calculation

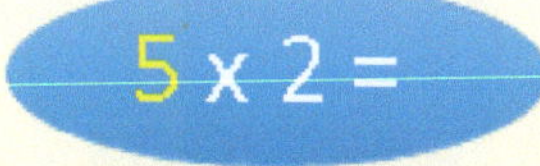

5 x 2 =	35
5 x 7 =	25
5 x 5 =	40
5 x 8 =	10
5 x 6 =	30

Multiple the number in the middle of each target by the numbers in the middle blue ring. Write your answers in the outside yellow ring.

Write the multiples of SIX in the blue jar and the non-multiples in the orange jar.

9   17   18   14   6   15   25   30   16   23   12   6   21   24

Fill in the blanks with the correct answers.

4 x 4 = _____   5 x 9 = _____   5 x 4 = _____

3 x 6 = _____   4 x 2 = _____   4 x 6 = _____

2 x 7 = _____   5 x 6 = _____   5 x 7 = _____

5 x 2 = _____   2 x 9 = _____   2 x 2 = _____

3 x 3 = _____   5 x 5 = _____   5 x 3 = _____

Match the right answer to each calculation

6 x 8 =

6 x 3 =

6 x 7 =

6 x 6 =

6 x 4 =

18

48

42

24

36

Multiple the number in the middle of each target by the numbers in the middle blue ring. Write your answers in the outside yellow ring.

Match the right answer to each calculation

Multiple the number in the middle of each target by the numbers in the middle blue ring. Write your answers in the outside yellow ring.

Match the right answer to each calculation

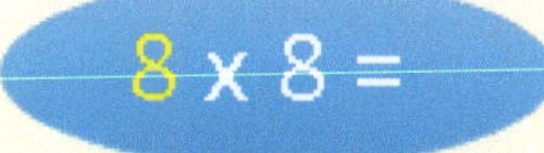

8 x 8 =	32
8 x 5 =	64
8 x 9 =	72
8 x 7 =	40
8 x 4 =	56

Multiple the number in the middle of each target by the numbers in the middle blue ring. Write your answers in the outside yellow ring.

Match the right answer to each calculation

Multiple the number in the middle of each target by the numbers in the middle blue ring. Write your answers in the outside yellow ring.

Match the right answer to each calculation

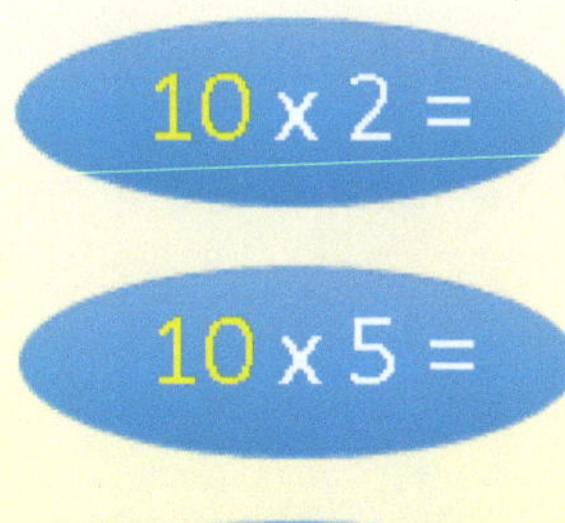

10 x 2 =   60

10 x 5 =   20

10 x 8 =   90

10 x 9 =   80

10 x 6 =   50

Multiple the number in the middle of each target by the numbers in the middle blue ring. Write your answers in the outside yellow ring.

Write the multiples of NINE in the blue jar and the non -multiples in the orange jar.

9 17 18 14 6 45 27 30 16 27 56 36 21 2

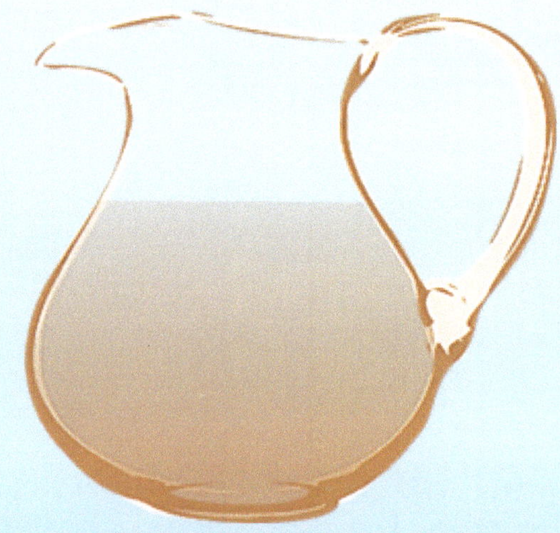

Fill in the blanks with the correct answers.

6 x 4 = _____	8 x 9 = _____	9 x 4 = _____
9 x 6 = _____	7 x 2 = _____	7 x 6 = _____
7 x 7 = _____	6 x 6 = _____	10 x 7 = _____
8 x 2 = _____	7 x 9 = _____	6 x 2 = _____
10 x 3 = _____	9 x 5 = _____	8 x 3 = _____

Match the right answer to each calculation

Multiple the number in the middle of each target by the numbers in the middle blue ring. Write your answers in the outside yellow ring.

Match the right answer to each calculation

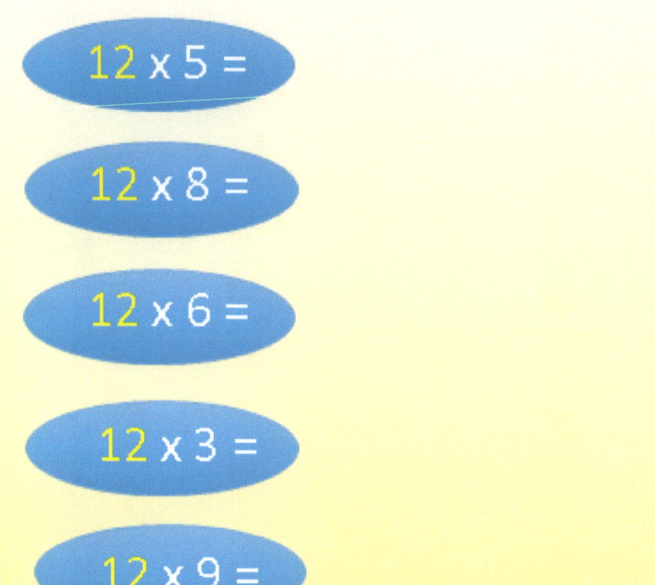

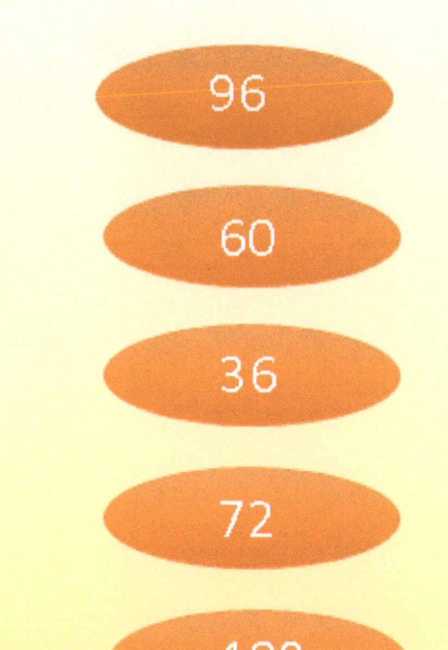

Multiple the number in the middle of each target by the numbers in the middle blue ring. Write your answers in the outside yellow ring.

Match the right answer to each calculation

Multiple the number in the middle of each target by the numbers in the middle blue ring. Write your answers in the outside yellow ring.

Match the right answer to each calculation

Multiple the number in the middle of each target by the numbers in the middle blue ring. Write your answers in the outside yellow ring.

Match the right answer to each calculation

Multiple the number in the middle of each target by the numbers in the middle blue ring. Write your answers in the outside yellow ring.

Write the multiples of 13 in the blue jar and the non-multiples in the orange jar.

39   24   117   114   65   52   92   107   78   104   68
117   92   107   78   91

Fill in the blanks with the correct answers.

14 x 4 = _____   13 x 9 = _____   13 x 4 = _____

13 x 6 = _____   14 x 7 = _____   14 x 6 = _____

12 x 7 = _____   15 x 6 = _____   15 x 9 = _____

15 x 2 = _____   12 x 9 = _____   12 x 2 = _____

11 x 3 = _____   15 x 6 = _____   14 x 3 = _____

Match the right answer to each calculation

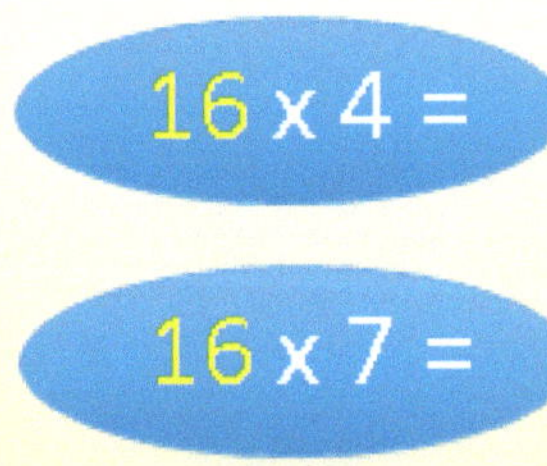

16 x 4 =	96
16 x 7 =	112
16 x 6 =	48
16 x 3 =	64
16 x 9 =	144

Multiple the number in the middle of each target by the numbers in the middle blue ring. Write your answers in the outside yellow ring.

Match the right answer to each calculation

Multiple the number in the middle of each target by the numbers in the middle blue ring. Write your answers in the outside yellow ring.

Match the right answer to each calculation

Multiple the number in the middle of each target by the numbers in the middle blue ring. Write your answers in the outside yellow ring.

Match the right answer to each calculation

19 x 3 =	152
19 x 7 =	57
19 x 9 =	133
19 x 4 =	76
19 x 8 =	171

Multiple the number in the middle of each target by the numbers in the middle blue ring. Write your answers in the outside yellow ring.

Match the right answer to each calculation

Multiple the number in the middle of each target by the numbers in the middle blue ring. Write your answers in the outside yellow ring.

Write the multiples of 17 in the blue jar and the non-multiples in the orange jar.

120   17   35   68   102   34   25   51   64   119   153
104   68   54   85   114   36   136

Fill in the blanks with the correct answers.

16 x 4 = ______   17 x 9 = ______   16 x 8 = ______
15 x 6 = ______   19 x 7 = ______   17 x 6 = ______
16 x 7 = ______   20 x 6 = ______   18 x 7 = ______
19 x 2 = ______   16 x 9 = ______   20 x 8 = ______
20 x 3 = ______   18 x 5 = ______   19 x 3 = ______